Yo-Yo World Trick Book

Featuring 50 of the Most Popular Yo-Yo Tricks
History of the Yo-Yo
Yo-Yo Families and How They Work

Harry Baier

DOVER PUBLICATIONS
Garden City, New York

introduction

A child lives through play, and toys are his world.

A child learns and develops his causal thinking by playing, as he begins to recognize cause and effect by the process of repeated patterns of play.

But playing isn't limited to children. Adults enjoy it too, especially in light of the constantly growing demands of working and everyday life. Adults learn by playing with toys and are thereby able to relax in a different way.

Preface

This book is dedicated to a toy that is known all over the world as "Yo-Yo." However, few people know what can actually be done with it. The Yo-Yo tricks taught in this book are intended to popularize the Yo-Yo and put an end to its time in the shadows. I underestimated the Yo-Yo because of its simplicity until I discovered the possibilities that the modern freewheeling Yo-Yo has to offer. Now I carry at least one of these spinning gadgets around with me everywhere I go.

Despite my love for Yo-Yo tricks, the simple up and down motion alone serves as a form of relaxation not to be taken lightly. It would be good for people the world over who are suffering from stress, to discover the calming and healing effect of this recurring movement.

The main advantage of the Yo-Yo is that it's small and easy to handle. You can take it anywhere and play with it almost anywhere too. For those with little time on their hands, a classic Yo-Yo is the best bet. But for me it's got to be a modern freewheeling Yo-Yo, as these provide the greatest variety of tricks.

Caution: if you use your Yo-Yo carelessly, you could cause injury to others. So always be careful when playing near others. Also, be careful when you're playing near glass or other breakable objects. Don't be like a bull in a china shop.

It is essential to check the Yo-Yo string before starting. A damaged string can cause harm to people and material, and it can destroy or impair the efficiency of your Yo-Yo.

Check the string by jerking it sharply.

A spare string can save you much grief in the long run. The worst accident I ever had with a damaged string happened to me when I was practicing "Reach for the Moon." The Yo-Yo hit me in the eye and I was knocked out. I was left with a black eye and considerably more respect for the Yo-Yo. The black eye healed quickly, but it was embarrassing having to explain how I got it! That's why:

Neatly performed tricks are guaranteed to find an audience.

A Yo-Yo is a toy for the young and old alike. A modern free wheeling Yo-Yo can defy the laws of gravity--at least visually. The number of tricks it can do is practically unlimited. In fact, I encourage you to send me any tricks that are not included in this book. Send them on video tape and I'll try to expand the collection of tricks in future editions.

I hope you'll have fun reading this book and learning all the tricks!

Finally, my sincere thanks to those untiring individuals who have helped me put this book together.

Joan Sallas i Campmany provided careful and time-consuming art work. He captured small details and had to learn some of the tricks himself to be able to do that. Now he also belongs to the family of Yo-Yo professionals.

I used Der Paradoxe Eierkocher by Wolfgang Bürger, Birkhäuser Verlag, Ch-4010 Basel, 1995, ISBN 3-7643-5105-5 for reference for "The History of the Yo-Yo" and "Yo-Yo Families and How they Work," with the kind permission of the publisher.

Christopher Toussaint chose the Yo-Yo as the subject for his academic thesis and checked my manuscript for accuracy.

Photos: Brigitta Koch, Jost Stober 1995 Freiburg

Thanks to: Petra Stephan, Angelika Ziegler, Horst Kolb and Thomas Rauser for their kind support.

THE HI
OF THE

Children were not the only ones playing with Yo-Yos in the early thirties when Yo-Yos first started in America.

STORY

The greatest Yo-Yo wave the world has ever seen spread from America to Europe.

That did not happen by chance. In fact, it was planned by a businessman named Donald Duncan, who sent his representatives all over the world...

...where they performed Yo-Yo tricks on street corners and in city squares. That took Yo-Yo fever to the limits. Yo-Yo marathons and even world championships were held at that time.

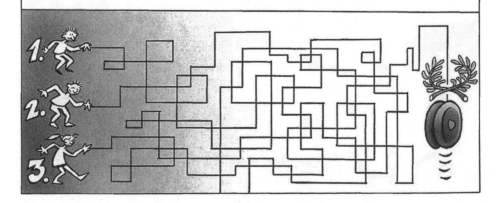

In the USA Duncan had entered into an alliance with the powerful newspaper magnate William Randolph Hearst. The deal was simple, yet brilliant.

Hearst advertised Duncan's Yo-Yos in his newspapers and anyone who wanted to take part in Duncan's Yo-Yo competitions had to enlist three subscribers for Hearst's publications. In 1931, that strategy sold three million Yo-Yos in the Philadelphia area alone in only one month!

The Yo-Yo is a device that stores kinetic energy in a revolving mass, which enables it to climb back up the string and perform many other tricks. In short, it is a flywheel...

...to play with. The actual concept of the flywheel is much older than the Yo-Yo itself. The potter's wheel, for example, was in existence in 5,000 BC.

And even in the Stone Age inventive craftsmen used a heavy stone with a hole in the middle to prolong the moment of inertia.

However, the flywheel served as the driving force behind a toy, before it was used in technology...

...to overcome the dead center of steam locomotives...

...stabilize the position of news satellites, (also to store power station energy and propel gyrobuses).

In the collection of the Berlin Antique Museum there is an Athenean dish dated 450 BC that depicts a youth playing with a Yo-Yo; evidence that the Yo-Yo was known in Ancient Greece.

We are unsure about the early history of the Yo-Yo. There are no signs that it was a Greek or Chinese invention. The Yo-Yo is said to have been invented in the Philippines in the distant past as a type of hunting weapon, a "Killer Yo-Yo" that would fit in well with modern science fiction.

It is said that a hunter would hide in the branch of a tree with a heavy stone and wait for his prey.

If he missed his target, he could easily retrieve his missile. However, one look at the design of a Yo-Yo challenges this wide-spread legend.

In the eighteenth century, the Yo-Yo appeared in England as a Chinese curiosity and became popular under the name of "bandilor," which could be traced back to the Indian city Bangalore.

According to a report in the Journal des Luxes in December 1791, the Yo-Yo came to Paris in October of that year as "joujou de Nomadie." (A. Fraser: Spielzeug. Oldenburg, 1966). It became extremely popular on the European continent within a very short period of time.

The contemporary French Yo-Yo titles "l'emigrette" and "coblentz" point to the great number of French aristocracy...

...who, in 1795, during the reign of terror of the Director, fled from France to Germany with their valuable Yo-Yos made of glass and ivory. (Le Clariétie: Les Jouets. Paris, 1894).

A print from the year 1792 shows a group of Yo-Yo players joining the allied forces. Among them is a soldier playing simultaneously with two Yo-Yos. (F.V. Grunfeld & E. Oker: Spiele der Welt. Frankfurt, 1976. Print copyright unknown).

One of the most prominent Yo-Yo players during Napoleon's time was Lord Wellington. (H. Volz: Introduction to Theoretical Mechanics, Volume 1, Frankfurt 1971).

The word Yo-Yo was probably coined and registered at the American Patents Office in 1930, by Donald Duncan. (F.M. Feldhaus: Die Technik - ein Lexikon. Munich 1970). The story of the Yo-Yo is the story of a simple toy that has enjoyed enormous success in the past, and is still going strong today!

For 54 years there were no significant changes in the construction of the Yo-Yo. Then in 1984 Michael Caffrey's Yo-Yo with a Brain was introduced into the market by YOMEGA Corp. It was developed to make Yo-Yo play easier to learn (which we will explain in more detail later). Fast spinning adjustable ball bearing Yo-Yos soon followed.

Yo-Yo Families:

By way of background, I'd like to describe in detail the different types of Yo-Yos. Practically speaking, there are three types of Yo-Yos. Each (apart from some "exotic" relatives) has a body and a slim shaft (or axle), which rolls up and down on a flexible string.

1. The Classic Yo-Yo (Up and Down)

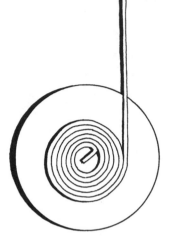

On a classic Yo-Yo, the end of the string is attached to the axle. When the string is fully unrolled, the Yo-Yo turns and starts its way back up to the player's hand. The thickness of the string influences the speed of the Yo-Yo in that the spool radius changes when the Yo-Yo rolls up and down. The complete volume of the string is minimal compared to the mass of the Yo-Yo body and thus is unimportant.

How it works:

When a classic Yo-Yo is rolled up, the string is wound around the axle and enlarges the diameter by two or three times. On the way down the spool diameter decreases and, therefore, the Yo-Yo speeds up. When the string is fully unwound, and the spool reduced solely to the axle, the Yo-Yo spins smoothly.

That is illustrated in this diagram of a falling Yo-Yo where the velocity of the Yo-Yo (v) is plotted over the fall (x). The phase curve of an academic Yo-Yo (see below) is a parabola open to the right. By

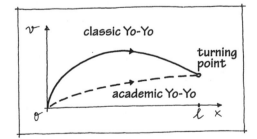

comparison, a classic Yo-Yo with the same axle diameter has a much higher speed when falling, and after peaking reaches the same final value as the academic Yo-Yo.

How classic Yo-Yos turn:

The classic Yo-Yo turns non stop when the string is unwound. The Yo-Yo movement can be most simply described as a jolt or a discontinuous change of speed from fall to rise.

After it turns, the Yo-Yo uses the energy stored in its flywhweel to rise again.

When the Yo-Yo is left to itself to fall and rise, it gradually loses energy like a bouncing ball. The Yo-Yo continually loses momentum due to friction caused by air resistance and the string rubbing against the side of the Yo-Yo. The Yo-Yo player replaces the lost energy by moving the Yo-Yo rhythmically via the string that is attached to his finger.

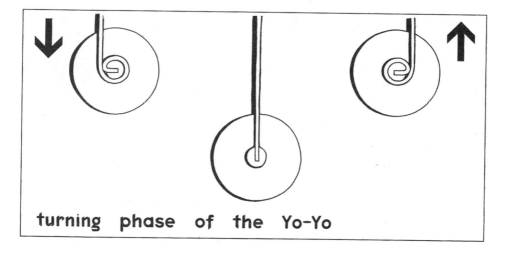

turning phase of the Yo-Yo

2. The Academic Yo-Yo:
(Maxwellian Wheel)

The difference between a classic Yo-Yo and an academic Yo-Yo is that the latter may have a string of any thickness and its spool radius stays the same when the string is wound and unwound (i.e. the string does not wind on top of itself). The Maxwellian Wheel is a type of academic Yo-Yo. It is hung on two strings that wind themselves around both sides of the flywheel in single loops.

How it works:

The spool diameter stays the same throughout the whole movement. Therefore, the fall and rise are uniformly accelerated. Unlike a free-falling object, the Yo-Yo is forced to turn by the string.

During this process the available energy is split: some of it is used up in the speed of the fall, the rest fuels the turn.

3. The Modern Yo-Yo:
(Freewheeling Yo-Yo)

The string on the modern Yo-Yo is looped around the axle in a noose. Both ends of the string meet at the end of the noose and are entwined to form a cord. This means that modern Yo-Yos can "sleep" or revolve freely in the noose when the cord is fully unwound (freewheeling Yo-Yo). This enables you to perform a number of tricks that are not possible with a classic Yo-Yo. The ability to sleep gives the modern Yo-Yo its special quality. Donald Duncan, with his highly developed sense of business, recognized that fact in 1931 and bought the idea from the Filipino Pedro Flores for $25, 000 (F.M Feldhaus: Die Technik - ein Lexikon. München 1970).

How it works:

A modern "sleeping" Yo-Yo works on the same principle as a gyroscope. The gyroscope effect keeps the Yo-Yo stable as it turns. It can sleep for only about one or two seconds after falling from a height of one meter. As most tricks require a longer sleeper, you must give the Yo-Yo a hefty swing on its way down to give it that extra drive.

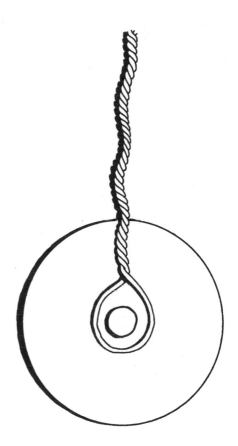

Practiced players can increase the revolving energy by 20 times and produce speeds of up to 140 revolutions per second. That is equal to a fall from a height of 25 meters. When it turns that fast, the edges of the Yo-Yo spin at nearly 100 km/h, which we call a really "long-sleeper." Even higher revolutions can be reached if the Yo-Yo is equipped with a ball-bearing axle.

A modern Yo-Yo enables you to store the energy he has generated in a sleeper and use it as needed.

There would be no point in a sleeping Yo-Yo that could not be awaken. You can wake your Yo-Yo by jerking the string . The Yo-Yo jumps slightly and its swiftly revolving body trap a short piece of the limp string as the string tightens up again. The string has a better hold on the body of the Yo-Yo then it does on a smooth axle, so the Yo-Yo winds itself back into your hand. By the way, you can also stop a Yo-Yo mid-fall and bring it back using the same method. You can see the trapped string if you carefully unwind it back to the spot, or unscrew the Yo-Yo halves.

Modern freewheeling Yo-Yos are a prerequisite for all the tricks in this book.

4. The YOMEGA with a Brain:

This Yo-Yo is a mixture of a classic and modern Yo-Yo. It has in its center a simple but helpful mechanism: a centrifugal clutch. When the clutch is engaged you have a classic Yo-Yo that only moves up and down. By giving the Yo-Yo a hefty spin, the clutch disengages through the rising centrifugal force and the YOMEGA becomes a modern long-sleeping Yo-Yo. Sleepers of up to 20 seconds are possible. As the centrifugal force decreases, the clutch re-engages at a certain point at which the YOMEGA, with still enough spin to spare, returns automatically to the hand. The springs inside the Yo-Yo are correspondingly preset. That's why it's called "the Yo-Yo with a brain." They are easy to handle and well-suited to beginners.

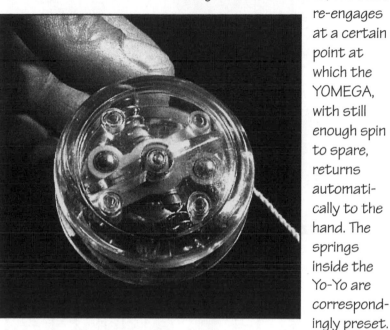

Yo-Yo Puzzle 1:

Now I want to pose a puzzle that you should be able to solve if you give it some thought.

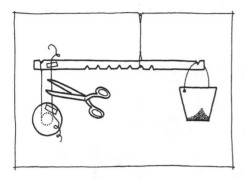

Attach a fully wound Yo-Yo to the left side of a scale and balance it out with a small bucket of sand.

Question: If you cut the thread fixing the Yo-Yo to the scale and the Yo-Yo starts to roll, does the scale hold its equilibrium? If no, which side of the scale sinks?

Solution: As the Yo-Yo gathers speed, the Yo-Yo side of the balance becomes lighter.

Yo-Yo Puzzle 2:

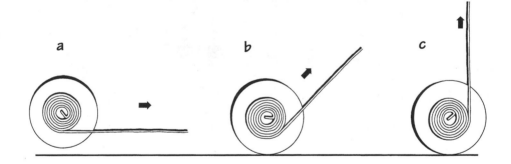

a   b   c

What happens when you slowly pull the string in the indicated direction?

Solutions:
a. The Yo-Yo moves to the right and winds up the string.
b. The Yo-Yo remains on the spot and the string is unwound.
c. The Yo-Yo moves to the left and the string is unwound.

Explanation of illustrations

Before we come to the Yo-Yo tricks, here are some additional bits of information:

● All tricks in this booklet are described for **right handed players.**

● **Important:** The hand to which the Yo-Yo is fixed is the throwing hand, the other hand is labeled "free hand" or "other hand."

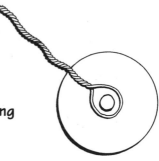

● **In order to master these tricks it is necessary to have a modern freewheeling Yo-Yo.**

● **Something happens with this finger.**

● **The string is depicted shortened.**

Changing the String and Adjusting its Length

1. Untwist the string and open the unwound string with your finger and thumb.

2. Thread the loop over the Yo-Yo and re-twist, smoothly.

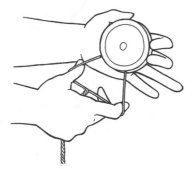

3. Length of string: the string should run from the ground to about three inches above your navel. After cutting the string to the proper length, tie a slip knot at the end of the string that attaches to your finger.

Tip

Change your string when it becomes dirty or no longer operates properly.

Changing the String (YOMEGA models)

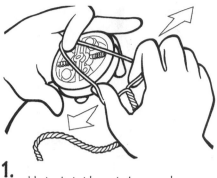

1. Untwist the string and open the unwound string with your finger and thumb.

2. Thread the loop over the Yo-Yo and turn your hand 180° in the direction of the arrow.

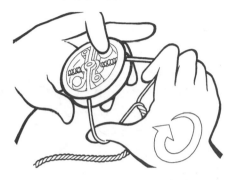

3. Cross threads....

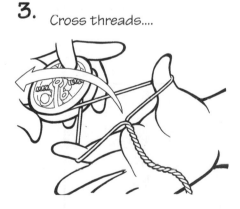

4. Thread the string over Yo-Yo a second time.

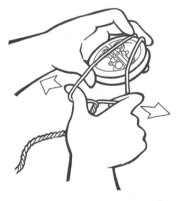

A second twist is necessary for some ball-bearing Yo-Yos like MOONSTAR, VIPER, YOMEGA FIREBALL and YOMEGA POWERSPIN. IMPORTANT: This process must be repeated for a **third time for the YOMEGA with a brain. The YOMEGA RAIDER and RBII require one loop only.**

Making A Finger Loop:

1. Open the loop at the end of the string and pull the string through loop.

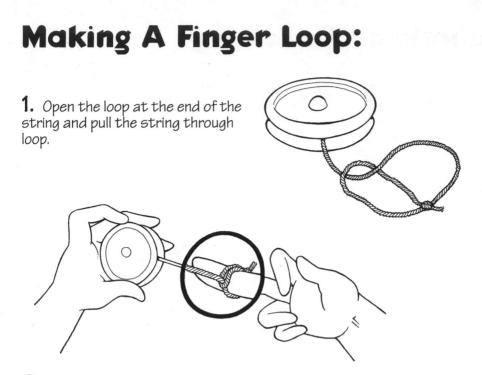

2. Slip the newly formed adjustable loop over your middle finger and tighten. Now the Yo-Yo is firmly in place.

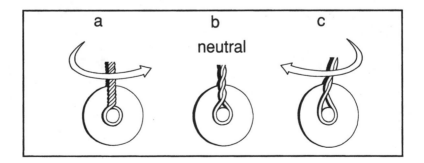

3. The string should be wound around the Yo-Yo axle so that it corresponds to illustration "b." If the string is too tight (illustration "a") the freewheeling action, called a sleeper, is not possible. If the string is too loose (illustration "c") then it is possible that the Yo-Yo will not awaken.

Winding the String

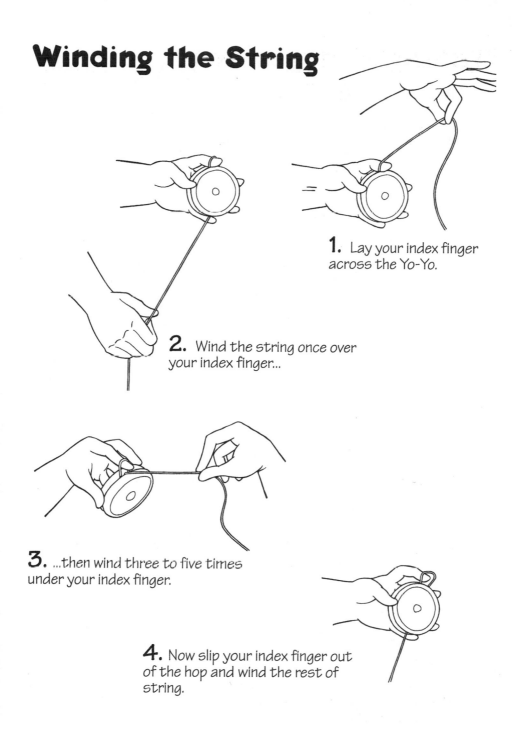

1. Lay your index finger across the Yo-Yo.

2. Wind the string once over your index finger...

3. ...then wind three to five times under your index finger.

4. Now slip your index finger out of the hop and wind the rest of string.

Winding the String
(Advanced Method)

1. Hold the Yo-Yo as shown.

2. Slot the Yo-Yo into the string at your throwing hand and hold.

3. Place your throwing hand below the Yo-Yo and your other hand above. Now slowly move the middle finger of your throwing hand upwards.

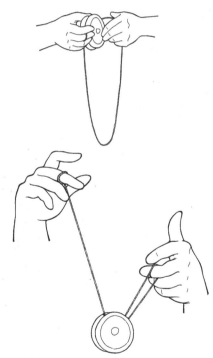

4. The Yo-Yo will rotate until it reaches your other hand, winding half of the string as it rotates. Drop the Yo-Yo and immediately tug it back to your hand to wind the remainder of the string.

Tip

A Yomega Brain Yo-Yo makes this maneuver simple to do. Also, winding the string in this way is a great trick in itself.

Yo-Olé!

Now You're Ready to Yo For it!

Basic Trick: The Sleeper

1. Hold the Yo-Yo in your hand, as shown. The string has to run above the axle so the string can unwind properly.

2. Curl your wrist and throw the Yo-Yo downward with power. Let the Yo-Yo roll out of your hand at about waist height, otherwise it will hit the floor. A strong spinning movement from the wrist is necessary for a long sleeper.

3. After throwing a sleeper, turn your hand 180° to catch the Yo-Yo.

4. With a gentle jerk of your middle finger on the string, the Yo-Yo returns to your hand.

 Tip

Practice until you can throw sleepers of ten seconds or longer. The longer, the better. When throwing fast sleepers, be careful the Yo-Yo doesn't return so quickly that it hurts your hand.

Walk the Dog

Throw a long sleeper. Gently lower the Yo-Yo to the floor. Walk with it and wake it up before it stops spinning.

The Creeper

This trick is similar to Walk the Dog, except instead of walking with it, crouch down and at the right moment wake it and whistle it back.

Spaghetti

Gather the string into small loops and hold them between your index finger and thumb until you have used up all the string. Drop it and wake it.

Around the Corner

Place the sleeping Yo-Yo over your shoulder and wake it.

Walk the Dog
(through the legs)

Walk the dog through your legs from behind you.

WOOF!

Surprise

1. Lift the sleeping Yo-Yo by its string...

2. ...and hold the string just above the Yo-Yo with your throwing hand...

3. ...now place the upper loop on your arm. Slowly lower the Yo-Yo and wake it before it runs out of momentum. The quicker it returns to your hand the better the effect.

Robin Hood

Let the sleeping Yo-Yo hang, and draw the string towards your body with your index finger and thumb. Optically a bow is implied. Aim and drop the Yo-Yo, which then returns to your hand.

Sky Rocket

1. While the Yo-Yo is sleeping, slip the string loop off your middle finger...

2. ...and throw it as high as you can. Catch the returning Yo-Yo in your hands or pocket.

Rock the Baby

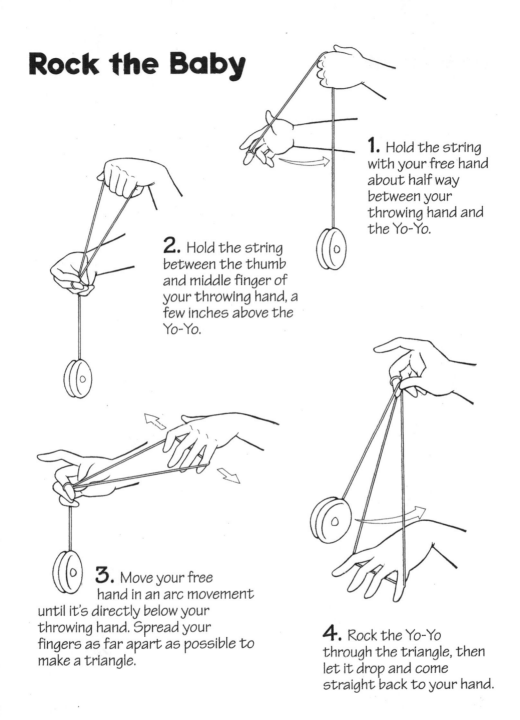

1. Hold the string with your free hand about half way between your throwing hand and the Yo-Yo.

2. Hold the string between the thumb and middle finger of your throwing hand, a few inches above the Yo-Yo.

3. Move your free hand in an arc movement until it's directly below your throwing hand. Spread your fingers as far apart as possible to make a triangle.

4. Rock the Yo-Yo through the triangle, then let it drop and come straight back to your hand.

Pinwheel Baby

Instead of rocking the Yo-Yo, give it a hefty swing. With an adequate sleeper you can perform many loops one after the other.

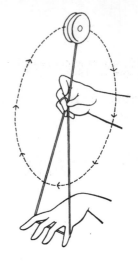

Dizzy Baby

Do a Rock the Baby and wind the string cradle...

...around the Yo-Yo. Let the Yo-Yo fall and...

...return to the hand.

Picture Tricks:

Note: Practice these tricks with your Yo-Yo *not* sleeping before you attempt them with a sleeper.

One-Handed Star

Carefully follow the diagrams and you'll have it!

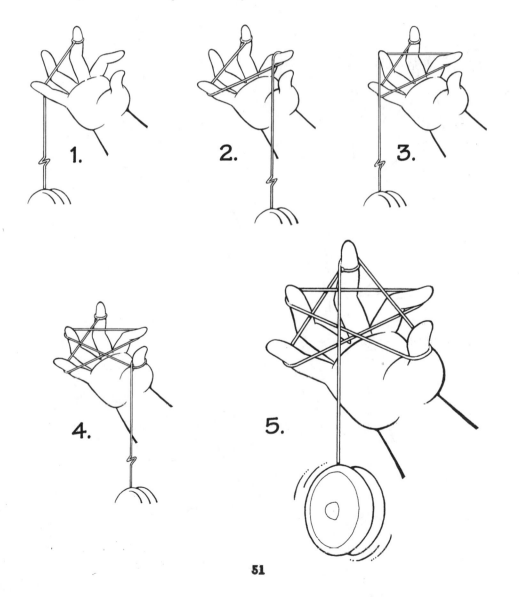

Texas Star

Note: These diagrams are drawn from the angle of the player.

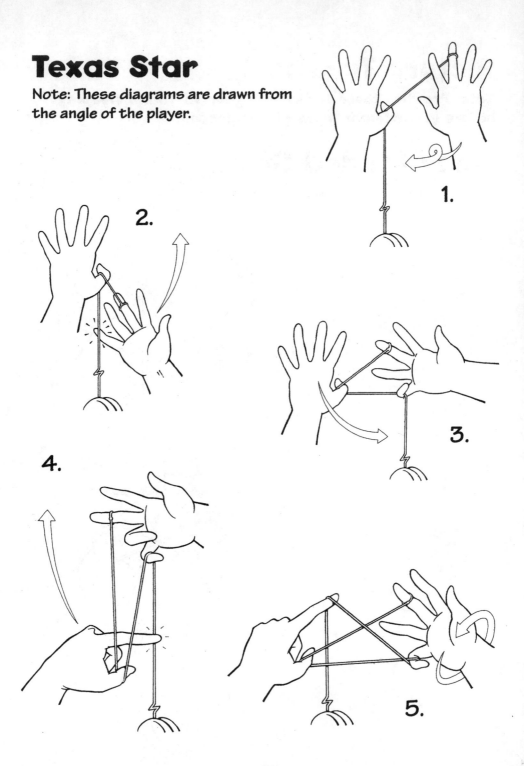

1.

2.

3.

4.

5.

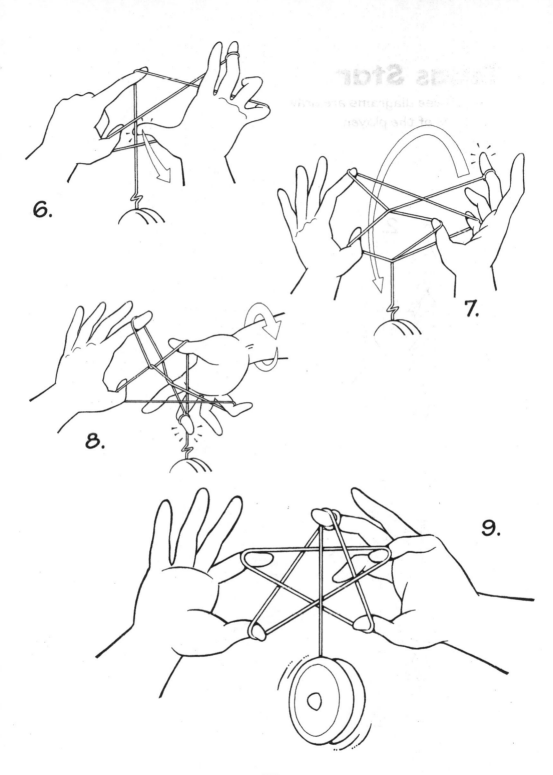

6.

7.

8.

9.

Eiffel Tower

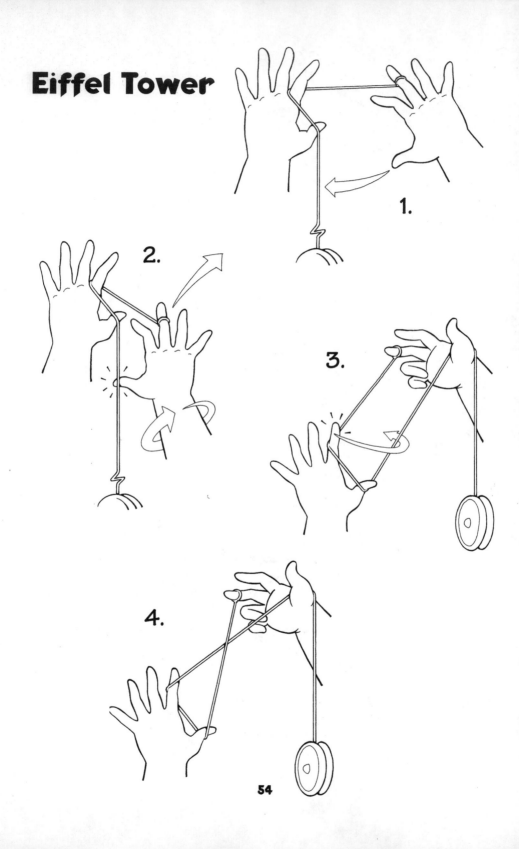

1.

2.

3.

4.

Pinch the string with the thumb and index finger of your left hand. While your throwing hand travels downward, let the string that is held at the side by the index finger and thumb of the left hand slide slowly downward.

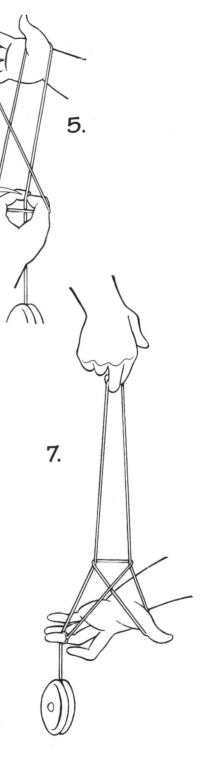

5.

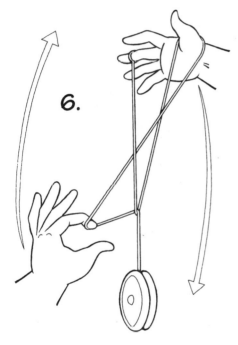

6.

7.

🎸 *Tip*

Practice until you succeed in making a tower. An upside down tower produces the letter "Y" as in Yo-Yo. By placing the Yo-Yo next to the "Y", you get the word "Yo".

Pro Tricks

Brain Twister

1. Throw a long sleeper. Place the string over the middle or pointer finger of your other hand and slowly raise your hand, as shown in the illustration.

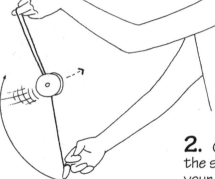

2. Gently slot the Yo-Yo onto the string halfway between your hands.

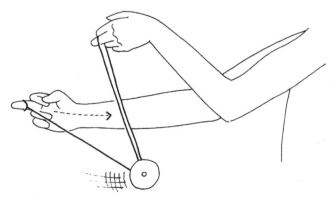

3. Make an arc around the Yo-Yo with your throwing hand.

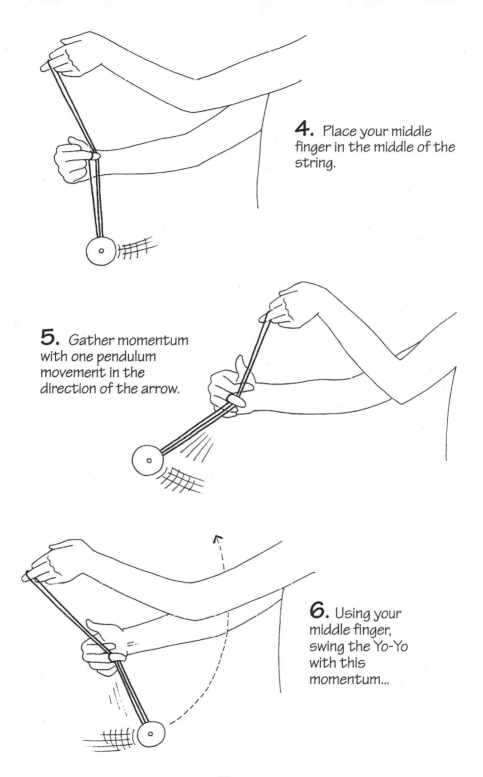

4. Place your middle finger in the middle of the string.

5. Gather momentum with one pendulum movement in the direction of the arrow.

6. Using your middle finger, swing the Yo-Yo with this momentum...

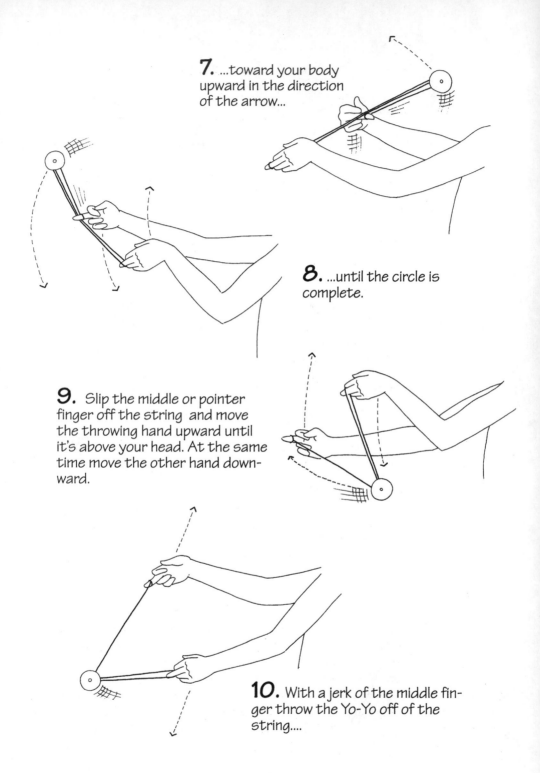

7. ...toward your body upward in the direction of the arrow...

8. ...until the circle is complete.

9. Slip the middle or pointer finger off the string and move the throwing hand upward until it's above your head. At the same time move the other hand downward.

10. With a jerk of the middle finger throw the Yo-Yo off of the string....

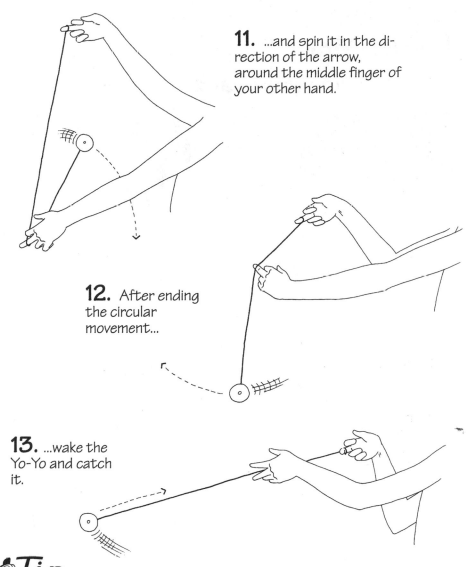

11. ...and spin it in the direction of the arrow, around the middle finger of your other hand.

12. After ending the circular movement...

13. ...wake the Yo-Yo and catch it.

Tip

Always try to keep your hands horizontal to one another. There shouldn't be too much friction between the Yo-Yo and the string, otherwise you'll run out of time before completing this really impressive trick.

It is important to gather momentum (step 5), and those of you who practice enough will soon be able to master several rotations. With each rotation the distance between the Yo-Yo and the throwing hand will become less and less as the string wraps itself around your finger. In order to complete this trick, simply let go of the string.

Front Mount
(forward and backward)

1. Throw a fast sleeper and move your throwing hand upward and hold the index finger of your other hand to the string about 3-4 inches above the Yo-Yo.

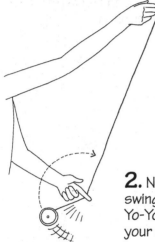

2. Now, with a swing, let the Yo-Yo spin around your index finger....

3. ...in order to slot it onto the string let the string relax a little as the Yo-Yo touches the string.

4. From here you can go into a Brain Twister, or reverse the rotation of the Yo-Yo by pulling upward with your throwing hand....

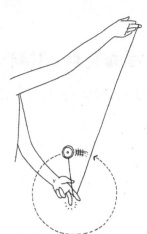

5. ...and with this momentum spin the Yo-Yo around the middle finger of your other hand.

6. When the rotation is complete catch the Yo-Yo on the string and give the string a bit of slack.

7. Then give the Yo-Yo a jerk with your other hand, throw it out and catch it.

Tip

The finger, acting as a pivot point, should be as near as possible to the Yo-Yo so the circle remains small and the trick is easier to learn.
Practice until you can throw the Yo-Yo directly from your hand into the front mount without any extra swings of the Yo-Yo at the end of the string.

Pinwheel

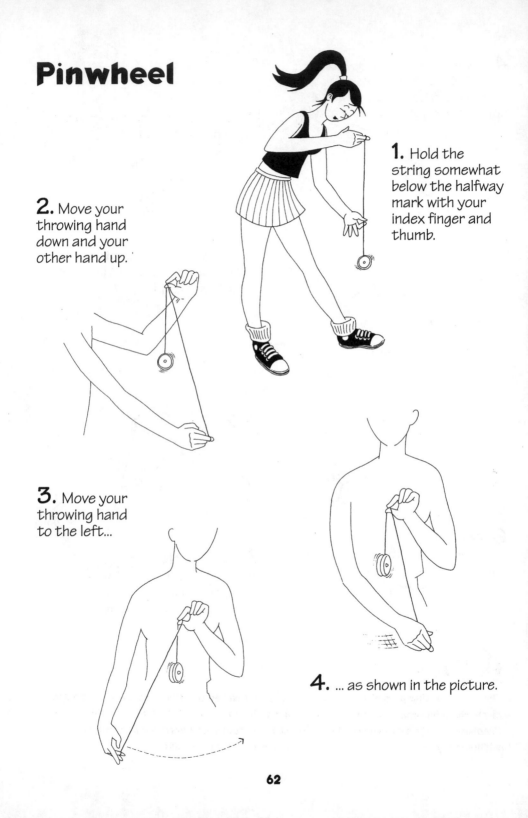

1. Hold the string somewhat below the halfway mark with your index finger and thumb.

2. Move your throwing hand down and your other hand up.

3. Move your throwing hand to the left...

4. ... as shown in the picture.

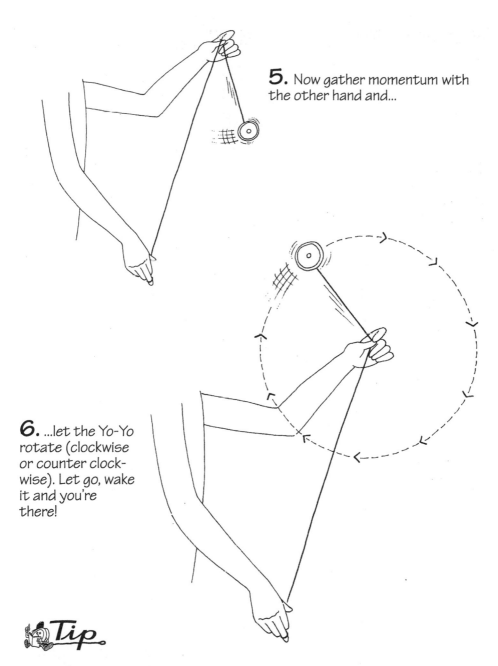

5. Now gather momentum with the other hand and...

6. ...let the Yo-Yo rotate (clockwise or counter clockwise). Let go, wake it and you're there!

Tip

Pinwheels can be performed in front of you or to your side. They are well suited as an introduction or finale to a Yo-Yo routine.

Rock the Baby in the Braintwister

1. This trick begins with a Front Mount. Let out string with your throwing hand while moving your other hand upward.

2. Lay your middle finger on the string. In addition, place the thumb of your other hand in the loop.

3. While keeping your throwing hand above, swing your other hand down in an arc, spreading your finger and thumb as far as possible.

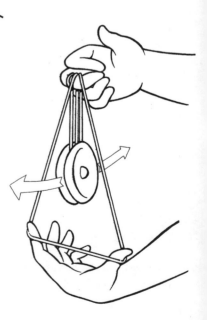

4. Swing the Yo-Yo to and fro as long as the sleeper will allow. Swing it once over your middle finger, then drop the Yo-Yo and retrieve it back to your hand.

Barrel Rolls

1. Throw a Front Mount. Place your throwing hand at the height illustrated, and place the string...

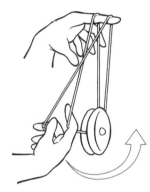

2. ...around the index finger of your other hand. At this point take the first string with the index finger of your throwing hand.

3. Let the Yo-Yo jump in the triangle by...

4. ...moving your throwing hand, with the gathered string, under the Yo-Yo. Withdraw your index finger and, if the Yo-Yo is still spinning fast enough, repeat the process.

Tip

Be careful not to touch the Yo-Yo, otherwise it will lose momentum. This trick is most effective when the Yo-Yo jumps several times in succession over your finger. For an attractive finale, don't withdraw your index finger at the last jump but, as in Brain Twister, place it onto the string and swing it so it rotates around the pivot of your other hand.

Side Throw

1. Hold the Yo-Yo as shown. The string must run above the axle, so it unwinds in the proper direction.

2. This is how you should position yourself.

3. Now with a hefty wrist spin throw an arc sideward.

Break Away

When the Yo-Yo reaches its highest point of travel, the Yo-Yo returns automatically to your hand. Yo-Yoers call this maneuver a Break Away.

Around the World

Using even more swing to make one or more complete rotations is called Around the World. This trick can also be executed to the side and in both directions: forward and backward.

Man on the Flying Trapeze

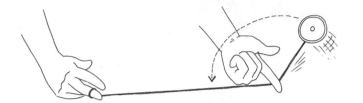

1. Begin with a strong Break Away. Make the circle smaller by using the index finger of your other hand as a pivot point.

2. The Yo-Yo wraps around your index finger and lands on the string. Let the Yo-Yo slide to the middle of the string by moving your hands closer together. Bounce it up and catch it.

Tip

As the Yo-Yo lands on the string, let the throwing hand give a bit so the Yo-Yo doesn't land too hard and start to wind. As in Front Mount, place your index finger close to the Yo-Yo so it makes a smaller arc.

As you become more proficient, add a few side Pinwheels before landing the Yo-Yo on the string.

Let the Yo-Yo stay on the string until the spin slows a bit. Otherwise after tossing it up, the Yo-Yo returns to your hand with full force.

Man on the Flying Trapeze
(backward)

1. From this position jerk your throwing hand to swing the Yo-Yo in a high arc...

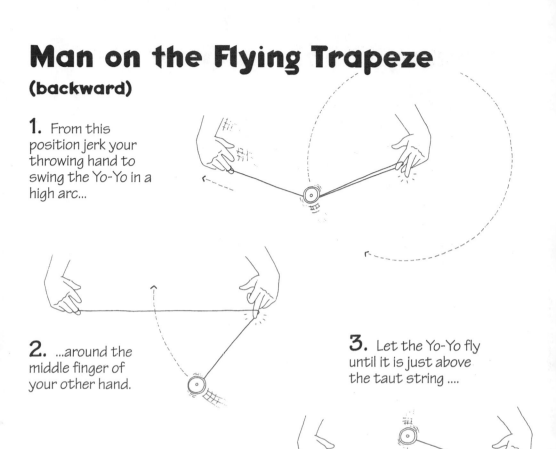

2. ...around the middle finger of your other hand.

3. Let the Yo-Yo fly until it is just above the taut string ....

4. ...and then gently land it onto the string. Bounce it up and catch it, or go into a reverse trapeze.

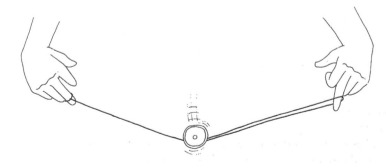

Monkey Climbs a Tree/ Elevator

Begin with a Man on the Flying Trapeze. Then move your throwing hand upward and your other hand downward. During this process your throwing hand must let out as much string as necessary until the rotating Yo-Yo nears it. Now slowly pull the string with your throwing hand. The Yo-Yo moves toward your other hand as if pulled by a ghost's hand. Toss it up and retrieve it. This trick has to be performed with a powerful sleeper.

Pendulum

After throwing a Man on the Flying Trapeze, the Yo-Yo is in the middle of the string. Move your hands toward each other until they touch. Gently swing the Yo-Yo to and fro until the sleeper begins to weaken. Throw the Yo-Yo upward and catch it.

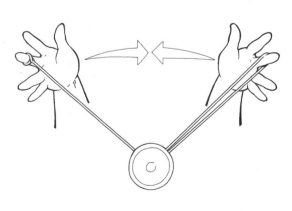

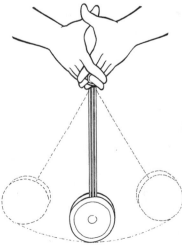

Around the World (small)

1. Place your hands together as in the Pendulum, and hang the string from your other hand over the middle finger of your throwing hand.

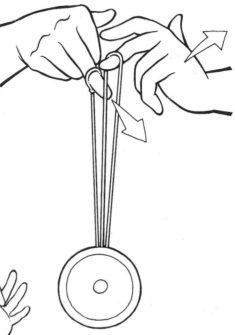

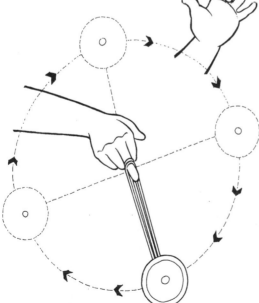

2. Take your other hand away and swing the Yo-Yo around your middle finger. Stop, throw and catch. A clockwise rotation works best but counterclockwise is also possible.

Rock the Baby in the Eiffel Tower

Drawn from the angle of the player

1. Begin with a Man on the Flying Trapeze.

2. Reaching between the strings with your thumb and index finger, grip the string of your throwing hand and hold it tight.

3. Move your throwing hand downward, placing the string over your ring finger. Move your hands in the direction of the respective arrows.

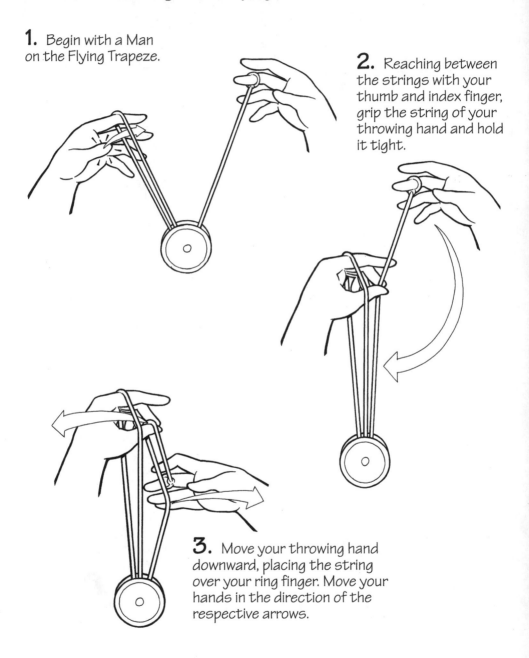

4. Gently slip the string off your thumb and index finger....

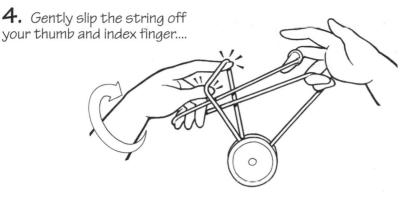

5. ...and place your thumb and index finger in the string and spread them.

6. Now carefully arrange the whole structure vertically.

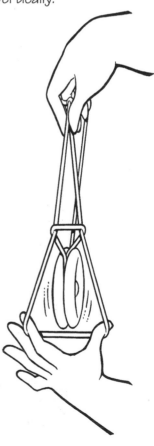

![Tip] **Tip**

To end the trick, drop the string gently with your other hand, then drop the string from your Yo-Yo hand. Be gentle or knots will result. For this trick a really long sleeper is necessary. At the very least, we recommend that you use a new string for your initial efforts. Create the triangle as late as possible, otherwise the Yo-Yo loses its rotation too quickly. You will need much practice to perform this trick perfectly.

Double or Nothing

1. This trick begins like Man on the Flying Trapeze but with even more spin, and the distance between your hands is less. Bring the index finger of your throwing hand into a position so the Yo-Yo can spin around it.

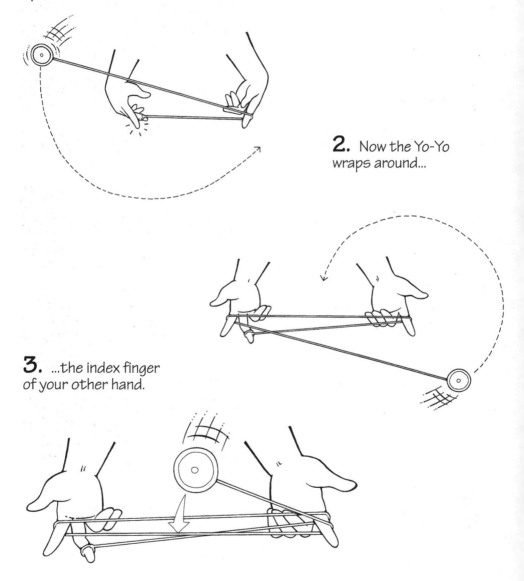

2. Now the Yo-Yo wraps around...

3. ...the index finger of your other hand.

4. Land the Yo-Yo onto the outer-most string, then take a deep breath. The first time it works is sensational!

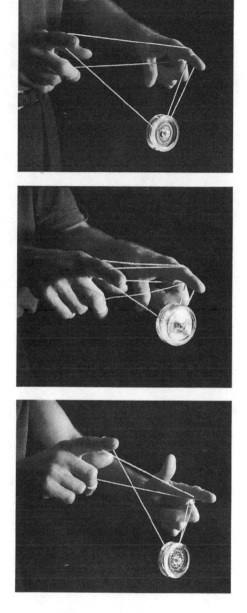

Triple or Nothing

Add another complete rotation to Double or Nothing. The next stage, and it is possible, is called "Quadruple or Nothing" (not pictured).

Middle or Nothing

Try to land the Yo-Yo onto the middle string instead of the outside string. You can also bounce from middle to outside and vice versa.

Tip

Whether the trick works or not largely depends on the distance between your hands. If it is too great, the string will be too short, and if it's too small, the Yo-Yo may collide with your throwing hand.

To increase the difficulty add a Lindy Loop (see page 80).

Windmill

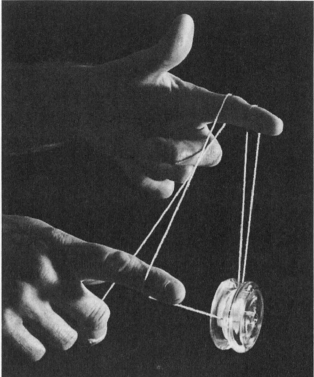

1. Start with a Double or Nothing.

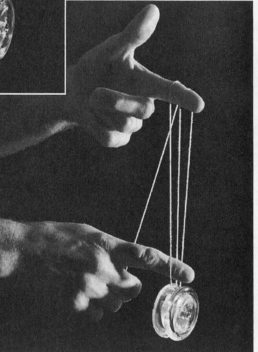

2. In this position simply withdraw the index finger of your throwing hand and...

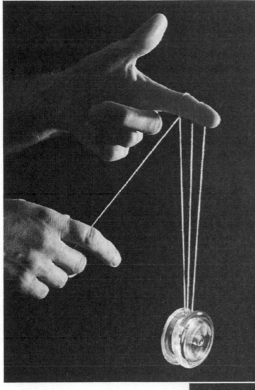

3. ...gather momentum and spin the Yo-Yo around the index finger of your other hand.

4. The result is a Man on the Flying Trapeze.

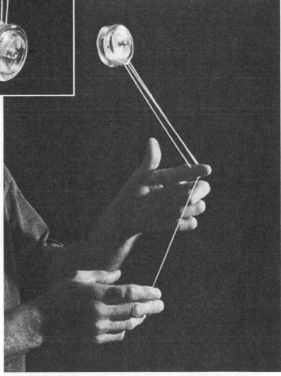

⚞Tip

Of course this maneuver also works with Triple and Quadruple or Nothing, but they must be spun two or three times around the hand. For Triple or Nothing, don't drop the string as in step 2, or the Yo-Yo will jump.

Man on the Flying Trapeze/ Trapeze with Back Flip (Lindy Loop)

Throw a strong Man on the Flying Trapeze, then rotate the Yo-Yo around your index finger and onto the string a second time.

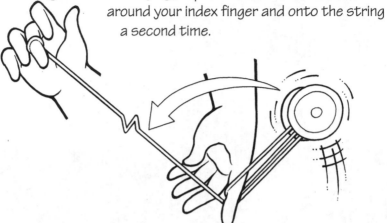

As you pull on the string with your throwing hand, the Yo-Yo rotates twice in the opposite direction around the index finger of your other hand. When the Yo-Yo reaches the top of its upward curve, let go and retrieve.

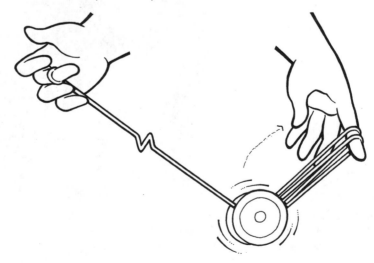

Lindy Loop Variation #2
Drawn from the angle of the player

1. Begin with Man on the Flying Trapeze. Hang the string - as in Small Around the World (page 71, picture 1). Move the index finger of your other hand downward toward the Yo-Yo.

2. Now gather momentum to spin the Yo-Yo over the pivotal index finger and land on the string.

3. Now very carefully let the string slip off the index finger of your throwing hand and the result is a Lindy Loop.

Tip

If the Yo-Yo drops on to the front string, you have a perfect Double or Nothing.

Lindy Loop Variation #3
Drawn from the angle of the player

1. Start as on the previous page. Move the other hand downward until the Yo-Yo is above your index finger...

2. ...jump the Yo-Yo over your finger and onto the opposite string. Complete this trick with a Small Around the world.

Tip

This trick looks simple at first but don´t be fooled. It should be done as quickly as possible so the Yo-Yo remains under control.

Dunk Shot

1. Place the string over your other hand as shown.

2. Using your throwing hand, place the string around the thumb and index finger of your other hand. Now grasp the string with your throwing hand...

3. & 4. ...pull the string and swing the Yo-Yo over your hand. If all goes well, the Yo-Yo will land on the middle string.

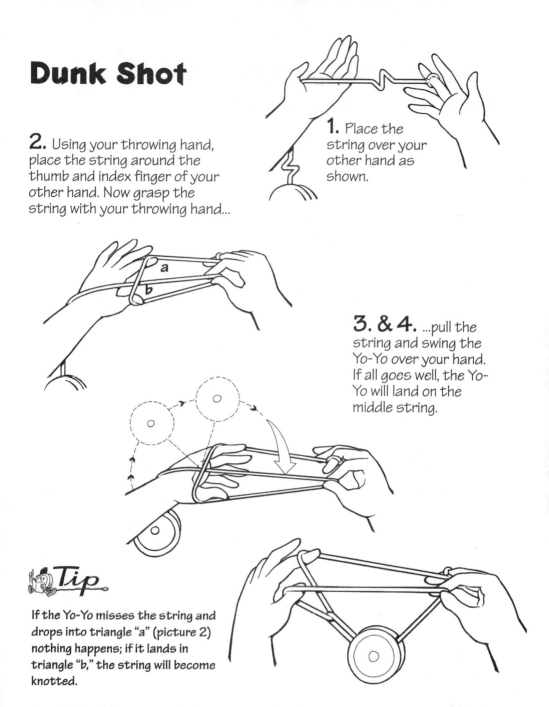

Tip

If the Yo-Yo misses the string and drops into triangle "a" (picture 2) nothing happens; if it lands in triangle "b," the string will become knotted.

Just for fun: After picture 2 shield the thumb and index finger of the other hand in such a way that the string cannot slip off, then start pinwheeling. Ending this trick with a pinwheel adds even more excitement to a great trick.

Sleeping Beauty or UFO

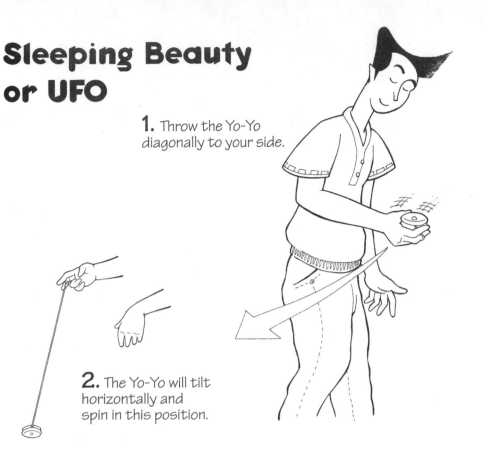

1. Throw the Yo-Yo diagonally to your side.

2. The Yo-Yo will tilt horizontally and spin in this position.

3. Raise the string carefully with the thumb and index finger of your other hand...

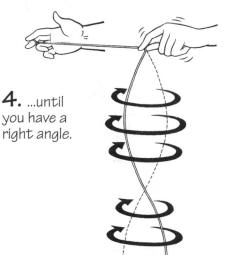

4. ...until you have a right angle.

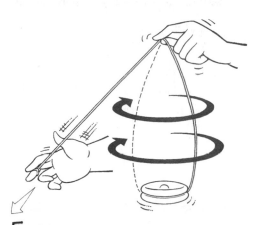

5. Pull on the string with your middle finger so the distance decreases between the other hand and the Yo-Yo.

6. Toss the Yo-Yo into the air with your other hand, and catch it.

Tip

This trick can also be thrown diagonally to the other side. It is also used to tighten or loosen the string.

Loop the Loop

This is certainly one of the most beautiful tricks, and can be mastered with adequate practice. But first, in order to understand the loop, a few physical things must be explained. It is a peculiarity of this trick that with every cycle the string winds or unwinds half a turn. This is achieved by the Yo-Yo's turning, so you can draw attention to the effect by using a Yo-Yo with two different colored sides.

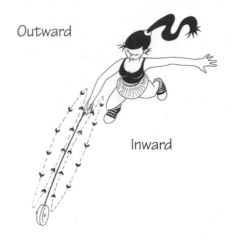

Outward

Inward

The direction of rotation depends on the way you play this trick and the hand you use.

Right handers who throw an inward loop loosen their string by half a turn per loop. On the other hand, an outward loop will tighten the string by half a turn.

Inward Loop

Left handers who throw an inward loop tighten the string by a half turn and with an outward loop loosen it.

Through careful observation we discover that these turns of the Yo-Yo take place at the back of the hand. At that stage of the trick the Yo-Yo has almost no velocity (self rotation) along the string, and is at that moment between winding up and winding out. The circling velocity on the other hand is at its maximum. The slight speed and therefore very limited self rotation of the Yo-Yo means a minimal gyro stabilization of the Yo-Yo axle. It is the maximum circling velocity, the swing of the hand and the pull of the middle finger for a new loop of the Yo-Yo, that turns it and prepares it for the necessary exiting position. But how does it perform this turn? The explanation is in the following picture. It shows that the turn is necessary for the trick to work properly.

Without the turning action, the Yo-Yo would be pushed instead of pulled every second time.

Pulling = right   Pushing = wrong

For the successful looping, the state of the string is important.

Luckily, physics automatically ensures the rendering of the turns with a fairly clean execution. Of course it depends on the right swing of the middle finger at the right time in order to complete a 180 degree turn.

Too tight   Just right   Too loose

With every loop the string tightens or loosens by half a turn. This means that a practiced player must know the state of his string. String that is too loose around the axle hardly permits looping. After 100 inward loops by right handers, the string is 50 rotations looser. Now it's easy to throw a sleeper but possibly the string is too loose for the Yo-Yo to return to the hand after sleeping. Now the string has to be tightened, which is most elegantly accomplished with a Sleeping Beauty.

String adjustments are necessary only when you're using a modern wooden or plastic Yo-Yo with a fixed axle. Simple modern Yo-Yos are good for looping because once you understand that the string can tighten or loosen itself, you can adjust the string correspondingly. Triple loop the string around the axle, or tighten the string as much as possible, so that a sleeper is almost impossible. Loops are also possible with classic Yo-Yos that don't sleep anyway.

With ball bearing or Yomega models, the string tightens or loosens when looping, but that doesn't affect the looping action of the Yo-Yo like it does with fixed-axle models. Consequently, you can do many loops without adjusting the string.

However, after many loops it is possible that the string could become so taut that the Yo-Yo itself would begin to rotate either clockwise or counterclockwise as you loop, which would make additional loops extremely difficult to control.

Basic Loop

Hold the Yo-Yo in your hand, as shown, taking care that the string is in the correct position.

The necessary swing comes from the wrist starting at hip height.

Before looping start with a...

Forward Pass

When the string is fully unwound, pull the Yo-Yo back to your hand and catch it.

Loop the Loop

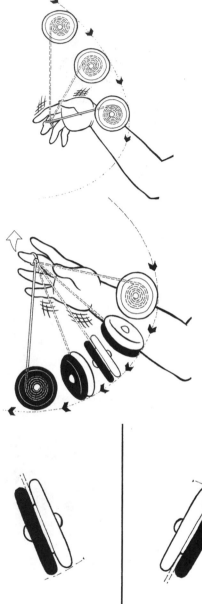

In principle, a loop is a repetition of Forward Pass without catching the Yo-Yo. This trick can be repeated as often as you like.

Instead of catching the Yo-Yo, let it circle past the inside of your hand....(inward loop)

....and exactly at this moment rotate your wrist, sending the Yo-Yo out again. The Yo-Yo will turn 180 degrees on its axis with every loop and will then be pulled by the string.

You can only control the looping Yo-Yo if it is slightly slanted.

From the players perspective, the Yo-Yo should be slanted to the right or to the left. Refer to the picture of the cowboy on page 10.

Left Handed

Right Handed

Two Handed

At the completion of the
loop, catch the Yo-Yo. As
soon as possible start
with two-handed loops like
the cowboy in the
preface.

Tip

The movement has to come from your wrist and middle finger. It definitely should
not be a locomotive motion of the hand and arm.
On August 23, 1975 Tony Flor did a record 7,531 loops.

Reach for the Moon

This trick is shaped like a "U." The Yo-Yo coming out of a loop is sent off above your head with a gentle flick of the wrist. This action requires very little energy. In position "a" the Yo-Yo is still 4-6 inches away from your hand, and it is exactly at this point that the wrist flick, either forward or backward, should happen.

Tip

This trick can also be played two-handed, and it can be repeated as often as possible. The secret is using little energy for the wrist flick.

Bank Deposit

Throw a sleeper in an arc between your legs. The string wraps around your thigh and lands in your trouser pocket. Everything must function perfectly for this trick to work. It helps to have trousers with high pockets so the Yo-Yo has easy entry.

String Jumping

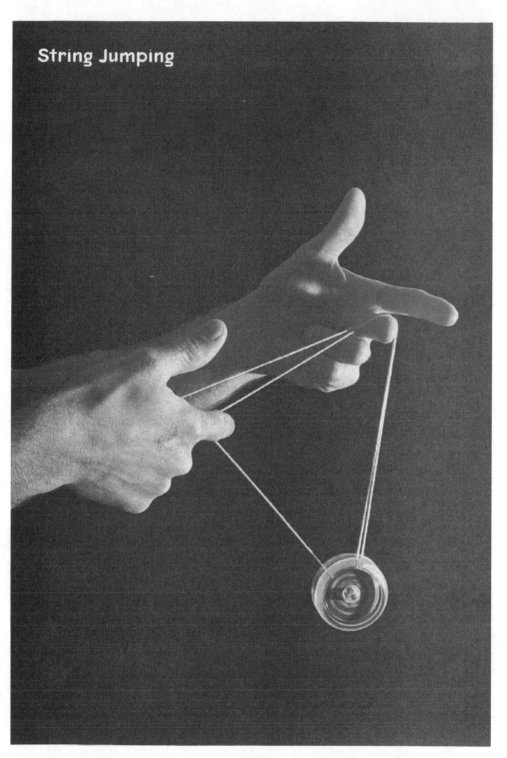

Rock the Baby in the Braintwister

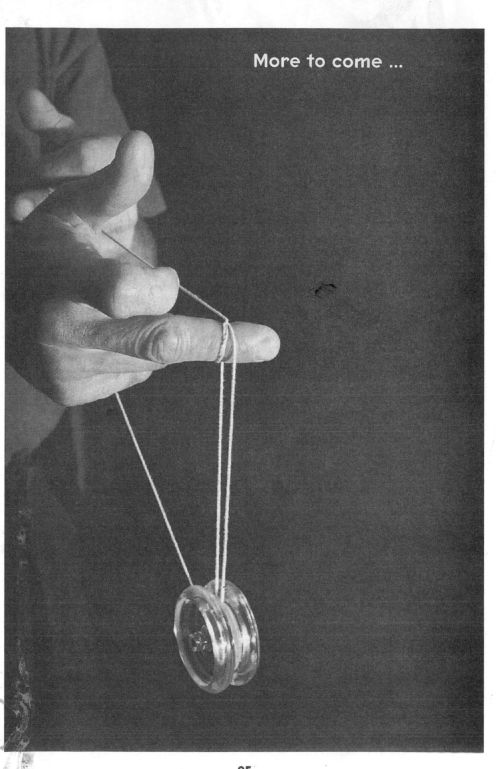

About the Author

Harry Baier was born in 1958 in Freiburg, Germany. In his early adult years he worked as a technician supporting computers and other office machines. He went on to form his own business and on one of his business trips he was fatefully introduced to the world of Yo-Yos from Yomega, Tom Kuhn, and BC.

He made his transition from computers to the world of Yo-Yos by leaving his company and becoming the manager at Active People, the main importers of Yo-Yos in Europe.

Ultimately, he was able to fuse his passion for the Yo-Yo with his creative and analytical skills to create his own product line CAME-YO which includes high-tech Yo-Yos called "Moonstar" and "Mondial." Yo-Yo players around the world know these Yo-Yos to be the "Rolls-Royce" of all Yo-Yos. Mr. Baier also teaches the sport of "Yo-ing" through classes and multi-media.